I0800002

U.S. PRESIDENTS MYTHS OR FACTS?

MYTHS AND FACTS ABOUT GEORGE WASHINGTON

EZRA E. KNOPP

PowerKiDS press

Published in 2024 by The Rosen Publishing Group, Inc.
2544 Clinton Street, Buffalo, NY 14224

Copyright © 2024 by The Rosen Publishing Group, Inc.

First Edition

All rights reserved. No part of this book may be reproduced in any form without permission in writing from the publisher, except by a reviewer.

Editor: Greg Roza
Book Design: Michael Flynn

Photo Credits: Cover Werkat/Shutterstock.com; (series background) Azamatovic/Shutterstock.com; pp. 5, 7, 11 Everett Collection/Shutterstock.com; p. 9 https://commons.wikimedia.org/wiki/File:Washington_1772.jpg; p. 13 https://commons.wikimedia.org/wiki/File:Birth_of_our_nation%27s_flag_-_C.H._Weisgerber._LCCN2004669130.jpg; p. 15 Vladimir Korostyshevskiy; p. 17 https://commons.wikimedia.org/wiki/File:White_House_1846.jpg; p. 19 (mule) slowmotiongli; p. 19 (American Foxhound) Mary Swift.

Library of Congress Cataloging-in-Publication Data

Names: Knopp, Ezra E., author.
Title: Myths and facts about George Washington / Ezra E. Knopp.
Description: Buffalo : PowerKids Press, 2024. | Series: U.S. presidents: myths or facts? | Includes index.
Identifiers: LCCN 2023032135 (print) | LCCN 2023032136 (ebook) | ISBN 9781499444056 (library binding) | ISBN 9781499444049 (paperback) | ISBN 9781499444063 (ebook)
Subjects: LCSH: Washington, George, 1732-1799–Juvenile literature. | Presidents–United States–Biography–Juvenile literature.
Classification: LCC E312.66 .K567 2024 (print) | LCC E312.66 (ebook) | DDC 973.4/1092 [B]–dc23/eng/20230712
LC record available at https://lccn.loc.gov/2023032135
LC ebook record available at https://lccn.loc.gov/2023032136

Manufactured in the United States of America

Some of the images in this book illustrate individuals who are models. The depictions do not imply actual situations or events.

CPSIA Compliance Information: Batch #CWPK24. For Further Information contact Rosen Publishing at 1-800-237-9932.

Find us on

CONTENTS

CHERRY TREES AND SILVER DOLLARS

Many people have heard the story that George Washington chopped down one of his father's cherry trees when he was a small child. When his father asked him about it, Washington said that he "could not tell a lie" and that he had chopped down the tree. His father praised his honesty.

What a great story! However, it's just a story. In 1800, writer Mason Locke Weems published a Washington **biography**—*The Life and Memorable Actions of George Washington*. The cherry tree story didn't appear in the book until the fifth edition came out in 1806.

IT'S A FACT!

WEEMS'S BOOKS WERE VERY POPULAR WITH CHILDREN ACROSS THE COUNTRY, WHICH LED TO THE POPULARIZATION OF THE CHERRY TREE STORY.

HISTORIANS HAVEN'T FOUND ANY **PROOF** THAT THE CHERRY TREE STORY IS TRUE. WHY WOULD WEEMS MAKE UP A STORY ABOUT A PERSON WHO'S ALREADY LARGER THAN LIFE?

MYTH OR FACT?

AS A YOUTH, WASHINGTON THREW A SILVER DOLLAR ACROSS THE POTOMAC RIVER NEAR HIS HOME.

MYTH

How far can you throw a flat rock? Can you throw it a mile (1.6 km)? Probably not! The Potomac River near Mount Vernon—Washington's family home—is more than 1 mile across.

This myth was likely started by Washington's step-grandson, George Washington Parke Custis. Custis once related that Washington had hurled a flat piece of slate, about the size of a silver dollar, across the Rappahannock River in Fredericksburg, Virginia. This seems more likely, but it has never been proven.

IT'S A FACT!

THE FIRST U.S. SILVER DOLLARS WERE CREATED IN 1794—LONG AFTER WASHINGTON WAS A YOUTH.

LIKE THE CHERRY TREE MYTH, THE SILVER DOLLAR MYTH HELPS SHOW WASHINGTON'S POSITIVE TRAITS. IT SHOWS THAT WASHINGTON WAS VERY STRONG.

WASHINGTON AT WAR

MYTH OR FACT?

WASHINGTON'S ACTIONS AS AN OFFICER FOR THE BRITISH HELPED START A WAR IN 1754.

FACT

In the mid-1700s, France and England both claimed land in the Ohio River valley. British forces warned French forces to leave—or they would be forced to leave.

In 1753, as an officer in the Virginia **militia**, Washington was sent to convince the French to leave. They refused. In 1754, Washington and his troops set up a base near Fort Duquesne. He led a surprise attack on the French forces in May, killing the commander. This was the beginning of the French and Indian War.

IT'S A FACT!

DURING THE FRENCH AND INDIAN WAR, NATIVE AMERICANS FOUGHT FOR BOTH SIDES. THIS WAS PART OF A LARGER WAR BETWEEN FRANCE AND ENGLAND (AND OTHER COUNTRIES) CALLED THE SEVEN YEARS' WAR.

THIS PAINTING BY CHARLES WILSON PEALE SHOWS GEORGE WASHINGTON WEARING AN OFFICER'S UNIFORM FOR THE FIRST VIRGINIA REGIMENT FROM THE FRENCH AND INDIAN WAR.

MYTH OR FACT?

WASHINGTON WON MOST OF HIS BATTLES AS A COMMANDER IN CHIEF OF THE COLONIAL FORCES DURING THE AMERICAN REVOLUTION (1775–1783).

MYTH

As leader of the colonial forces, Washington was very good at **discipline** and encouraging his men. These qualities helped him find early success against the British in Boston, Massachusetts.

However, Washington wasn't a good **tactician**. Thomas Jefferson once said that Washington often "failed in the field." Despite these drawbacks, Washington remained passionate about his command. He inspired many soldiers and kept the numbers of soldiers high. He often demanded better supplies and more food for his men.

IT'S A FACT!

WASHINGTON WAS GOOD AT INSPIRING HIS MEN, BUT HE USED THREATS TO KEEP THEM IN LINE AS WELL. HE HAD **DESERTERS** AND THIEVES FLOGGED, OR BEATEN.

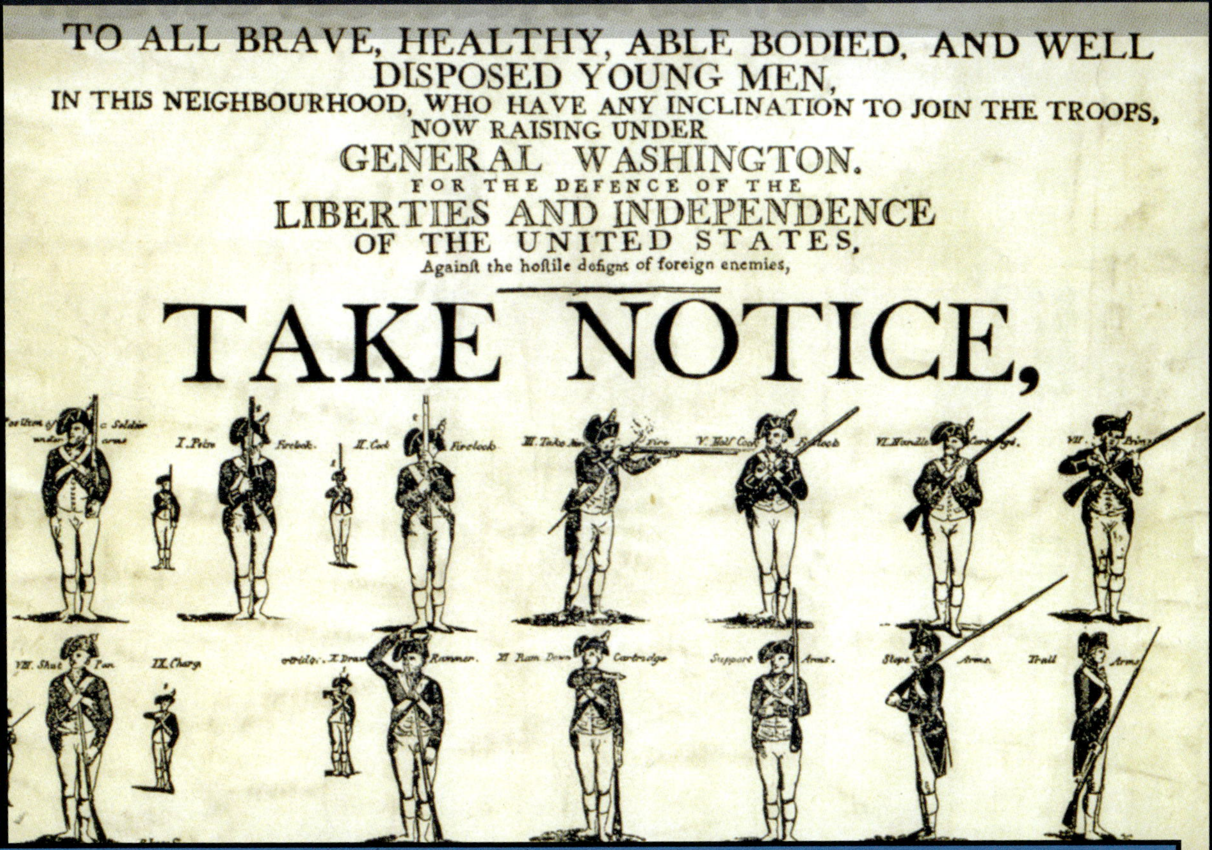

HISTORIANS HAVE POINTED OUT THAT WASHINGTON LOST MORE BATTLES THAN ANY OTHER SUCCESSFUL GENERAL IN HISTORY. HOWEVER, IT WAS WASHINGTON'S SUCCESS IN BUILDING AN UNDERGROUND SPY NETWORK THAT HELPED THE COLONIES WIN THE WAR.

MYTH OR FACT?

GEORGE WASHINGTON ASKED UPHOLSTERER BETSY ROSS OF PHILADELPHIA, PENNSYLVANIA, TO CREATE THE FIRST FLAG OF THE UNITED STATES.

MYTH

History books have long suggested that Washington and Ross discussed the flag before she created it. However, while historians know that Ross did in fact make flags during the American Revolution, there's no proof that she made the first American flag design.

This story arose in the late 19th century, many years after the deaths of Washington and Ross. In 1873, Ross's grandson spoke of the story. Soon after, it was published in *Harper's Monthly*.

HISTORIC RECORDS SHOW THAT WASHINGTON SPENT SOME TIME IN PHILADELPHIA IN 1776. HOWEVER, THERE'S NO **EVIDENCE** THAT HE EVEN MET BETSY ROSS.

MYTH OR FACT?

WASHINGTON KNELT IN PRAYER IN THE SNOW AT VALLEY FORGE.

MYTH

Washington and thousands of colonial soldiers spent the winter of 1777 to 1778 in Valley Forge, Pennsylvania. They had few supplies. Many soldiers didn't even have shoes. However, one of Washington's greatest accomplishments was inspiring his men to carry on despite the terrible conditions.

There's a famous story that says a man came upon Washington kneeling in the snow, praying to God to help his army **persevere**. This is another story first related by Weems in his biography of Washington. It likely never happened.

HISTORIANS THINK WEEMS ADDED THE STORY ABOUT WASHINGTON KNEELING IN THE SNOW TO MAKE THE STRUGGLE FOR FREEDOM SEEM LIKE A **DIVINE** MISSION FOR COLONIAL SOLDIERS.

AT HOME WITH THE PRESIDENT

MYTH OR FACT?

WASHINGTON NEVER LIVED IN THE WHITE HOUSE.

FACT

Washington became the nation's first president in 1789. Not long after, plans to build the "President's House" near the Potomac River began to take shape. Construction began in 1792 and didn't conclude until 1800. Second U.S. president John Adams and his wife, Abigail, were the first presidential family to live in the White House.

During his eight years as president, Washington and his wife, Martha, lived in New York and Philadelphia. After, Washington returned to his family home, Mount Vernon.

WHITE HOUSE 1846

WHILE IN OFFICE, PRESIDENT WASHINGTON SIGNED A BILL TO ESTABLISH A PERMANENT U.S. CAPITAL ON THE POTOMAC RIVER. THIS CITY CAME TO BE NAMED AFTER THE NATION'S FIRST PRESIDENT.

MYTH OR FACT?

WASHINGTON WAS A TALENTED DOG BREEDER.

FACT

Dogs were used for many purposes in colonial America. They helped with farming and hunting. Reports show that Washington enjoyed fox hunting, and he kept a kennel of dogs that he visited frequently. The dogs he kept included English foxhounds, greyhounds, mastiffs, pointers, and other breeds.

Washington bred hunting dogs for speed. His friend (and fellow officer during the American Revolution) Marquis de Lafayette sent Washington several French staghounds. They were big, active dogs. Washington bred them with his dogs, creating the American foxhound.

IT'S A FACT!

WASHINGTON IS ALSO CREDITED AS AMERICA'S FIRST MULE BREEDER. MULES WERE IMPORTANT FARM ANIMALS IN THE UNITED STATES FOR MANY YEARS.

THE AMERICAN KENNEL CLUB (AKC) RECOGNIZES WASHINGTON AS THE "FATHER OF THE AMERICAN FOXHOUND." IT ALSO REPORTS THAT HE LIKELY HELPED TO DEVELOP OTHER AMERICAN DOG BREEDS, INCLUDING THE BLUETICK COONHOUND AND THE AMERICAN ENGLISH COONHOUND.

NO HIGHER RANK

In 1775, the **Continental Congress** made Washington the general and commander in chief of the army of the "United Colonies." For eight years as president, Washington was also commander in chief of U.S. armed forces. In 1798, President John Adams gave Washington the **unique** rank of lieutenant general and commander of the U.S. Army, which he held until his death in 1799.

In 1976, President Gerald Ford promoted Washington to the rank of general of the armies of the United States. This is the highest rank in the U.S. military, and no one will ever reach a higher rank than George Washington.

WASHINGTON'S TIMELINE

FEBRUARY 22, 1732	WASHINGTON IS BORN IN WESTMORELAND COUNTY, VIRGINIA.
1743	WASHINGTON'S FATHER DIES. HIS OLDER HALF-BROTHER LAWRENCE TAKES HIM IN.
1748	WASHINGTON BEGINS WORK AS A LAND SURVEYOR (SOMEONE WHO MEASURES AREAS OF LAND).
1752	WASHINGTON STARTS LEASING, OR RENTING, MOUNT VERNON. HE INHERITS IT IN 1761.
1759	WASHINGTON MARRIES MARTHA DANDRIDGE CUSTIS.
1775	WASHINGTON IS NAMED COMMANDER IN CHIEF OF THE COLONIAL FORCES.
1778–1779	WASHINGTON AND HIS TROOPS SPEND A BITTERLY COLD WINTER IN VALLEY FORGE.
OCTOBER 19, 1781	BRITISH TROOPS SURRENDER TO WASHINGTON IN YORKTOWN, VIRGINIA, ENDING THE AMERICAN REVOLUTION.
APRIL 30, 1789	WASHINGTON BECOMES THE FIRST U.S. PRESIDENT.
DECEMBER 14, 1799	WASHINGTON DIES AT MOUNT VERNON.

GLOSSARY

biography: The story of a person's life.

Continental Congress: A series of groups (congresses) held by leaders in the American colonies during the time around the American Revolution.

deserter: Someone who leaves the military illegally.

discipline: Control gained by enforcing order.

divine: Of, relating to, or coming directly from God or a god.

evidence: Something that shows that something else is true.

militia: A group of people who aren't an official part of the armed forces of a country but who are trained like soldiers.

persevere: To keep at something in spite of difficulties.

proof: Something showing that something is true.

tactician: One skilled in tactics, or methods of using forces in combat.

unique: Special or different from anything else.

upholsterer: Someone who is trained to use fabric, padding, springs, and other materials to create furniture.

FOR MORE INFORMATION

BOOKS

Harrison, Wag. *The Presidents Did What?* Richmond, VA: Belle Isle Books, 2021.

Huddleston, Emma. *George Washington.* Mendota Heights, MN: North Star Editions, 2023.

Regan, Michael. *George Washington and the American Presidency*. Lake Elmo, MN: Focus Readers, 2018.

WEBSITES

George Washington
kids.nationalgeographic.com/history/article/george-washington
Find out even more about the first U.S. president with National Geographic.

George Washington's Mount Vernon
www.mountvernon.org
This website is packed with information about Washington and his family home.

Publisher's note to educators and parents: Our editors have carefully reviewed these websites to ensure that they are suitable for students. Many websites change frequently, however, and we cannot guarantee that a site's future contents will continue to meet our high standards of quality and educational value. Be advised that students should be closely supervised whenever they access the internet.

INDEX

TITLES IN THIS SERIES

MYTHS AND FACTS ABOUT
ABRAHAM LINCOLN

MYTHS AND FACTS ABOUT
GEORGE WASHINGTON

MYTHS AND FACTS ABOUT
JOHN F. KENNEDY

MYTHS AND FACTS ABOUT
THEODORE ROOSEVELT

MYTHS AND FACTS ABOUT
THOMAS JEFFERSON

MYTHS AND FACTS ABOUT
ULYSSES S. GRANT

ISBN: 9781499444049

9 781499 444049

PowerKiDS press

DID YOU KNOW? WONDERS OF THE WORLD

20 THINGS YOU DIDN'T KNOW ABOUT

THE COLOSSEUM

ELEANOR BRADSHAW